TITLE: THE PERILS OF CARELESSNESS

NEGLECTING YOUR CUSTOMER' NEEDS

Felecia.B.Brown

CONTENT

Chapter 1: Figuring out your customer's requirements.

Chapter 2: Developing a positive attitude towards customers.

Chapter 3: Customers First.

Chapter 4: Creating an amazing customer experience.

Chapter 5: knowing your customer's necessities.

Chapter 6: Managing losing a customer.

Chapter 7: Kinds of customer's necessities.

Chapter 8: Results of indiscretion.

Chapter 9: How would you defeat a customer's Indiscretion

Chapter 10: conclusion

About The Author (Felecia.B.brown)

Felecia.B.Brown, a seasoned business strategist and consumer behavior expert, is the brilliant mind behind the thought-provoking book "Neglecting Your Customer's Needs." With a career spanning over two decades in the corporate world, felecia.b.brown has earned a reputation for her insightful perspectives on customer relations.

Felecia's journey began as a frontline customer service representative, allowing her to witness firsthand the impact of neglecting customer needs. Fueled by a passion for improving customer experiences, she ascended through the ranks, eventually becoming a sought-after consultant for major corporations.

In her book, Felecia combines real-world anecdotes with meticulous research, dissecting the consequences of neglecting customers in a fast-paced business environment. Her writing transcends traditional business literature, offering a refreshing blend of practical advice and empathetic understanding.

Felecia.B. Brown challenges businesses to rethink their customer centric strategies, emphasizing the long-term benefits of prioritizing customer needs. Her work serves as a wake-up call for organizations, urging them to bridge the gap between customer expectations and the services they provide.

As a thought leader, Felicia .B. Brown continues to influence the business landscape, advocating for a customer first approach. "Neglecting Your Customer's Needs" stands as a testament to her commitment to fostering positive relationships between businesses and their most valuable asset—the customer.

INTRODUCTION

In the fast-paced landscape of business, where competition is fierce and demands are ever-changing, overlooking the needs of your customers can have severe consequences. Carelessness in understanding and addressing customer requirements not only jeopardizes client satisfaction but also erodes trust, hindering long-term success. In this exploration, we delve into the ramifications of neglecting your customers' needs and the pivotal role attentive customer care plays in fostering lasting relationships.

CHAPTER 1: FIGURING OUT YOUR CUSTOMER'S REQUIREMENTS.

Understanding and addressing your customer's conditions is an abecedarian aspect of fostering successful connections and delivering value in any professional setting. It involves a multifaceted approach that combines effective communication, active listening, and a keen mindfulness of the customer's pretensions and prospects. To begin with, effective communication forms the bedrock of figuring out your customer's requirements. Establishing an open and transparent channel of communication allows for the freedom of information, icing that both parties are on the same runner.

This involves not only conveying your ideas easily but also laboriously harkening to the customer's enterprises, preferences, and objects. Through this exchange, a comprehensive understanding of the customer's conditions begins to take shape. Active listening is a pivotal element of this process. It goes beyond hearing words; it involves interpreting the nuances, understanding the underpinning provocations, and discerning implied prospects. By attentively harkening to your customer, you can gain perceptivity into their challenges, bournes , and unique perspectives. This information becomes inestimable in acclimatizing your approach to precisely meet their requirements. Also, grasping the broader environment of your customer's assiduity and request is essential. A deep understanding of the external factors impacting their business allows you to anticipate requirements, identify implicit challenges, and offer visionary results. This mindfulness positions you as a strategic mate, contributing not only to immediate requirements but also to long- term success. The process of figuring out your customer's conditions also involves asking the right questions. By probing into specific inquiries about their objects, precedences, and constraints, you demonstrate a commitment to delivering acclimatized results. These questions should be thoughtful and probing, designed to prize detailed information that goes beyond face- position considerations. In addition to direct communication, using technology and data analytics can enhance your capability to understand customer requirements. exercising client relationship operation (CRM) systems, tracking stoner geste , and assaying request trends can give precious perceptivity. These tools empower you to make informed opinions and recommendations grounded on concrete data, aligning your strategies more nearly with your customer's prospects. In exibility is another crucial element in the process of figuring out customer conditions. Feting that requirements may evolve over time, being adaptable to changing circumstances demonstrates your commitment to delivering ongoing value. Regular checks ways and feedback sessions help ensure that you stay attuned to any shifts in precedence's or arising challenges. The establishment of clear prospects from the onset is pivotal. easily needed design reaches, timelines, and deliverables give a solid frame for collaboration. This not only helps help misconstructions but also sets the stage for a more effective and productive working relationship. Eventually, the capability to gore out your customer's conditions is an ongoing, dynamic process. It requires a combination of interpersonal chops, assiduity knowledge, technological, and Characters, commitment to nonstop enhancement. By investing time and trouble in understanding your guests deeply, you won't only meet their immediate requirements but also place yourself as a trusted mate in their long- term success. Empathy, frequently hailed as the capability to understand and partake the passions of another, emerges as the foundation of guests' understanding.

the significance of cultivating compassionate practices, enabling businesses to perceive their guests not as deals but as individualities with distinct requirements, preferences, and feelings. Social harkening One of the primary benefits of social listening is the capability to gain deep perceptivity into client preferences, opinions, and actions. By assaying exchanges, businesses can identify what guests love, dislike, and desire. This real- time feedback provides a window into the customer mind, enabling companies to conform their products, services, and communication strategies consequently, Social listening is an important radar for detecting trends and arising motifs within your assiduity. By staying attuned to the conversations passing across social platforms, businesses can identify shifts in consumer interests, anticipate request demands, and place themselves as originators within their eld. This visionary approach allows companies to stay ahead of the wind in an ever- changing geography. Guests appreciate brands that hear, Social listening facilitates active engagement with the followership by responding to commentary, addressing queries, and admitting positive feedback. This not only fosters a sense of connection but also demonstrates a commitment to customer satisfaction, potentially turning guests into brand advocates. Effective guests understanding begins with active listening. It's not simply about hearing words but decoding the nuances, relating pain points, and discerning the underpinning provocations. Through active listening, businesses gain perceptivity that goes beyond the face, paving the way for acclimatized results that address the core requirements of their guests. In the intricate cotillion of business, understanding and meeting client needs stand as pillars of enduring success. The trip from a transactional exchange to a profound client- business relationship begins with the delicate art of knowing your client's requirements. This comprehensive disquisition seeks to unravel the layers of this art, examining the multifaceted approaches, challenges, and transformative impact that arise from a deep understanding of guests' conditions. Knowing your customer needs transcends the connes of a one- time sale. It involves structure connections that extend beyond the point of trade. This relational approach enables businesses to evolve with their guests, anticipating changing requirements, and getting trusted mates in their trip. Understanding guests needs goes hand in hand with delivering a lawless client experience. Whether online or offline, the entire guest's trip should be orchestrated to feed their requirements painlessly. This holistic approach not only satisfies immediate conditions but also contributes to long- term client satisfaction and fidelity.

CHAPTER 2: DEVELOPING A POSITIVE ATTITUDE TOWARDS CUSTOMERS.

developing a positive and professional customer service station is to understand your customers and their requirements, prospects, and feelings. You can do this by harkening laboriously, asking open concluded questions, empathizing, and showing respect. Try to understand the customer's point of view and issues, and put all the sweat into fixing the problem. Avoid transferring customers to multiple service professionals, because it can be frustrating having to repeat information.

Customer stations are a compound of a person's beliefs, passions, and behavioral intentions toward your business. These stations are frequently formed based on a mix of factors. Particularly influential that play a considerable part in developing and solidifying certain stations. Being authentic and honest is extremely important. Customer's can spot an insincere person immediately. However, they will generally repay the positive station and are more likely to trust the staff and the business, If the customer gets genuine and sincere relations from a customer service platoon member It will be an impressive one.

It's no secret that customer service can have a profound and continuing effect on the customer experience with a company. Given that customer service as a part is demanding, annoyances and vexation are part of the everyday operations for the service staff, and it becomes indeed more imperative to remain positive while dealing with customers. Customer's anticipate high norms of service and top class experience with a company every time and through every touch point. Creating similar positive tests for them is possible by maintaining a positive station in customer service, along with empowering CSRs with the right information at their fingertips. This combination can be hard to cultivate.

It's important for a company to give training and coaching to help the customer service staff understand the significance of a positive station & give tools like interactive decision trees to help deliver the right information to customers. There are several examples of how decision trees contribute to a positive station among call center agents by furnishing structure, commission, effectiveness, and thickness in their relations. These tools not only ameliorate the client experience but also produce a more positive and probative work terrain for the agents themselves.

The reason for a positive station in customer service (and in every aspect of life) is that such a station spreads and has a profound positive effect on people. By remaining positive, the service brigades would be suitable to mould customer gest and impact them a lot more fluently. It's necessary for the service staff to concentrate on the good effects and positive relations they've with guests, rather than on only some of the negative bones that may do. By maintaining a positive station in customer service, the service staff would set the tone for all their relations with their guests, which would 'rub off' on the guests too. The fact is that when service staff focus on the bothered, irked, and screaming guests only they encountered during a workday, the result is a feeling of dread and languor that will unmask over to the coming day, making them detest coming to work. These negative stations also snowball, and the service staff would conceivably come rude a positive station in customer service is simply about remaining calm during relations, making every effort to make robust connections with customers and icing, so that they can view the company as authentic through Positive station and Product Knowledge.

In the quest for a positive attitude, challenges are inevitable. Negative reviews, customer complaints, and unforeseen issues can cast a shadow on even the most positive interactions. However, it's essential to view these challenges as opportunities for growth. Addressing concerns with grace, learning from feedback, and demonstrating a commitment to improvement can turn negatives into positives. It's a testament to resilience and an unwavering dedication to customer satisfaction.

The Power of a Smile: It's Contagious

A smile: It's the simplest yet most potent tool in the arsenal of positive customer interactions. When a customer is greeted with a genuine smile, it sets the tone for the entire exchange. Smiles are infectious, creating a ripple effect that transcends the initial interaction. Imagine walking into a store and being met with a beaming smile – suddenly, the environment feels warmer, more welcoming.

In a world where transactions are increasingly digital and impersonal, the value of human connection cannot be overstated. A positive attitude towards customers is the bridge that transforms a mere transaction into a relationship. Customers are not just faceless entities with wallets; they are individuals with unique needs, preferences, and stories.

Positive Attitude and Word of Mouth: Word of mouth has always been a potent force in shaping a business's reputation, and a positive attitude is it's catalyst. When customers feel genuinely valued and appreciated, they become advocates. They share their positive experiences with friends, family, and even strangers, becoming ambassadors for the brand.

In the excellent embroidery of business, an uplifting outlook towards customer's arises as a string that weaves enduring associations. A mentality stretches out past overall revenues and quarterly reports, rising above the conditional idea of trade. Developing an uplifting outlook is an interest in connections, a pledge to compassion, and an acknowledgment of the human component inside each customer's

As organizations explore the intricacies of the cutting edge commercial center, the persevering through effect of inspiration turns into a directing light. It's an update that behind each buy, survey, or communication, there's an individual looking for an item or administration as well as an encounter that reverberates on a more profound level. In the ensemble of trade, an uplifting outlook is the tune that changes the common into the remarkable, leaving an amicable reverberation that waits in the hearts of customers.

CHAPTER 3: CUSTOMERS FIRST

Putting your customers first is running a company that makes guests feel special. Suppose of it as a business mindset that promotes a positive customer experience at every step of the customer trip. Every time you make a business decision, consider how it'll affect your customers. Customer-centric strategy is an approach at which a company anticipates its customer demands and promotes an astral experience at each touchpoint. It helps nurture the culture of pious guests and eventually increase gains. Such a plan implies creating services that would go over and beyond customer's prospects. It boosts a brand's value in the guests' eyes. Being customer- acquainted helps make palm- palm connections between a customer and a company. The client's first strategy requires ample trouble. What does it take to put guests first in the long run?

✓ Cultivate all-hand support: There are some companies around the globe that make their internal societies just about covering customer's satisfaction. Only support agents should be responsible for what the druggies suppose. Is it right? Wrong. A customer first strategy won't work if it falls solely into customer- facing workers' hands. Your business is about to profit if you grow a customer service mindset inside marketing, deals, or IT brigades. A world- notorious fast food eatery McDonald's is a pictorial illustration of a company promoting each- hands support. Its workers switch duties to reach the loftiest productivity and understand guests more. For example, a principal director can be a cashier to load off the associates in busy hours and not let guests leave. Yes, everyone is OK about being at the counter once in a while. By having different brigades aiding guests at some point, there's a chance to hear what a customer thinks and wants.(everything from proper office installations to redundant day- offs will do) happy staff frequently leads to indeed happier guests. And product brigades, in their turn, have to gather customer point requests and make sure every detail is enforced.

✓ Promote translucency: People generally want their questions answered right down. The further they stay, the further they get angry and bothered. sorely enough, it's not always possible to address each client's complaint due to some reasons. Believe it or not, a ' customer comes first ' policy can occasionally be mischievous. When you ca n't deliver guests what they ask for, consider giving them a clear reason why it's that. To put it simply, handle the situation with translucency. Guests like being heard, so let them know what obstacles you have right now and when their request will be filed down. As scary as the whole idea of translucency may feel, it 'll be a perfect element for your customers first strategy.

✓ Pitch ideas to ameliorate: customer experience, suppose if you produce a popular product or service, it's time to relax a bit. Well, it doesn't work that way. You can't just sit back and watch deals rise on their own. For starters, it's important to use your stylish trials to enjoy the topmost results. Plus, guests will feel your eschewal and might get angry. Your challengers won't lose their chance; they will come up with innovative ideas to invite your guests down. Innovation is the form for an important customer- centric strategy. It shows you realize the guests' needs and are ready to feed them no matter what. Not to be taken suddenly, look for some fresh ideas to ameliorate customer witness, it 'll indicate your devotion to service quality and products.

✓ Celebrate success: erecting a customer first strategy can be really challenging for your customer support platoon. It means that service agents need to be at the top of their game regularly, so you can find new ways to impress your guests. Workers say that giving credit for good work is important. So, as a business proprietor or a platoon lead, you should incentivize great performance and celebrate success. It's essential to bandy collective pretensions and make reaching the company's mileposts. You also can stroke your workers on the reverse for achieving customer service. A customer acquainted gospel is n't only a good thing to exercise, but it's essential to retaining customers. Now, people trust businesses that appreciate them and center around their requirements. A united platoon, translucency, innovative ideas, and understanding of customer demands can be game- changing, making your customer service exceptional.

In the heartbeat of any successful business, there's a rhythm that echoes loud and clear: "Customers First." It's not just a catchphrase; it's a guiding principle that transforms transactions into meaningful connections. Picture this: a world where every decision, every innovation, and every interaction is orchestrated with the customers, they are the lifeblood of any business. It's about recognizing their needs, understanding their pain points, and genuinely caring about their journey. When customers become the focal point, every aspect of the business aligns to enhance their experience. It's a philosophy that goes beyond profit margins and market share, reaching into the hearts of those who fuel the business – the customers. The enduring impact of putting customers first isn't just measured in transactions; it's measured in the relationships built, the trust earned, and the positive influence that reverberates in the marketplace.

CHAPTER:4 CREATING AN AMAZING CUSTOMER EXPERIENCE.

In the bustling marketplace where options abound and choices are abundant, creating an amazing customer experience isn't just a business strategy; it's an art form. It's about transcending the transactional and weaving a tapestry of interactions that leaves customers not just satisfied, but genuinely delighted. through the realms of customer experience, exploring the elements that transform an ordinary interaction into an extraordinary memory. Creating an amazing customer experience begins with understanding the customer's journey from start to finish. It's about more than just the moment of purchase; it encompasses every touchpoint, from the first awareness of the product or service to post-purchase engagement. Businesses that excel in customer experience take a holistic approach, mapping out the entire journey to identify opportunities for enhancement.

•The Power of First Impressions: Setting the Stage, they say you never get a second chance to make a first impression, and in the realm of customer experience, this couldn't be truer. The initial interaction sets the stage for the entire journey. Whether it's a website visit, a phone call, or a walk into a physical store, the first impression lingers in the customer's mind. Businesses that prioritize creating an amazing experience ensure that the first encounter is not just smooth but leaves a positive imprint.

•Building Trust: Trust is the currency of customer experience. Businesses that prioritize open and transparent communication build a foundation of trust with their customers. This involves not just sharing information about products or services but being candid about policies, pricing, and potential challenges. When customers feel informed and confident in their interactions, trust flourishes. Businesses that communicate openly create an environment where customers feel valued and respected.

•Feedback: is a valuable resource in the journey of creating an amazing customer experience. Businesses that welcome and learn from feedback demonstrate a commitment to continuous improvement. Whether it's through surveys, reviews, or direct customer communication, gathering insights allows businesses to refine their strategies, address pain points, and enhance the overall experience.

A culture of learning from feedback is a key driver in staying attuned to evolving customer expectations. In the strong space of Business, the journey for a momentous customer experience is like making a gem. It's a puzzling dance where every co -activity, from the basic touch highlighting post purchase responsibility, adds to the propelling story of shopper steadfastness.

One size fits none, particularly in customer's collaborations. An inspirational perspective stretches out to customizing the customer's experience. It includes perceiving and recognizing individual inclinations, recollecting past communications, and fitting administrations as needs be. Personalization isn't just about customization; it's tied in with showing customers that they are seen and esteemed as exceptional people. Going above and beyond in this manner is a sign of organizations that focus on certain customer's connections.

10 Ways in creating an amazing customer's experience ✓ Realize the Power of the Customer Experience Mindset.

✓ Build a Customer-Centric Culture.

✓ Develop Customer-Focused Leadership.

✓ Design a Zero-Friction Customer Experience.

✓ Create Customer Experience-Focused Marketing.

✓   Leverage Technology to Make Customers' and Employees' Lives Easier and Better.

✓   Define Your Code on Ethics and Data Privacy in Customer Experience.

✓   Send a thank-you note.

✓   Eliminate long hold times.

✓   Send a surprise "gift" when your customers are least expecting it.

the pursuit of an extraordinary customer experience is not merely a business strategy; it's an ongoing commitment to the beauty of genuine connections. It's an ode to the artistry of crafting moments that transcend the transactional, leaving a lasting legacy of satisfaction, loyalty, and positive word of mouth. Continuous improvement, driven by feedback, ensures that businesses evolve with the changing expectations of their customers. The frontline ambassadors—employees—play a pivotal role, infusing positive energy into interactions. Surprise and delight, exceeding expectations, become the magic that leaves an indelible mark on the hearts of customers.

CHAPTER 5: KNOWING YOUR CUSTOMER'S NECESSITIES.

Knowing and understanding customer's needs is at the focal point of each and every effective business, whether it sells straightforwardly to people or different organizations. When you have this information, you can utilize it to convince potential and existing clients that purchasing from you is to their greatest advantage.

Understanding customer's needs is a significant piece of any business. By understanding what your customer needs, you can more likely design essentially every part of your business, particularly your advertising system. Customer's needs are the inspiration driving a customer's dynamic interaction. The customer's craving drives them to buy an item and to pick that item over another. Organizations concentrate on their customer's necessities to give better items, showcasing methodologies and customer's care.

There are basically two kinds of customer needs:

•physical

•mental.

These necessities frequently cross-over, which at times makes it trying to isolate them.

Physical requirements: are the easiest to distinguish, as they frequently have direct arrangements. For instance, on the off chance that somebody is eager, they need something to eat.

Mental necessities: are at times harder to distinguish, however they are likewise ordinarily the more remarkable driver of customer choices. For example, A physical need tells a customer they need something to eat, a mental need guides them towards food that furnishes them with a particular inclination. Mental requirements can be the contrast between a Customer purchasing a serving of mixed greens over a burger since they need to feel great.

To more readily grasp the customers' requirements, think about both their physical and mental necessities. A few normal sorts of customer needs include: Value: An item that squeezes into their own financial plan

Experience: A charming encounter while utilizing the item

Capability: An item that tackles a particular issue for the customer

Feeling: A particular inclination the customer can have, while utilizing your item

Similarity: An item that functions admirably with different items your customer's utilizes

Individual: An individual encounter the customer has while interfacing with a brand or reaching customer's support.

Social: An item that accompanies societal position, like purchasing the furthest down the line model vehicle to intrigue colleagues.

To comprehend your customer' necessities, you really want to initially comprehend who your customer is. You can begin by creating a purchaser persona, which is a made up depiction of your ideal customer, in light of examination and your ongoing customer base. It portrays the kind of individual your business requests to, including their possible age, orientation, area, pay and side interests.

With an itemized purchaser persona, you can contemplate the requirements of that crowd. For instance, an interest group of ladies in their 50s might have unexpected requirements in comparison to men in their 20s. A purchaser persona assists you with remembering your ideal customer as you are exploring and characterizing their requirements in later stages.

Customer necessities and consumer loyalty can be considered as something that is at the focal point of each and every effective business. Each business needs motivation to be at the top.

High consumer loyalty can assist with drawing in new business, help maintenance, and increment deals among your current Customer base. As a matter of fact, 73% of business pioneers report an immediate connection between their client support and business execution, as indicated by Zendesk's 2022 CX Patterns Report. Individuals love to adhere to what they're generally OK with. In this way, it's important that you constantly track down ways of matching customer assumptions as these permit you to increment customer faithfulness and fulfillment, contact another crowd, and lift deals.

•Steadfastness: Is Important Organizations never again need to simply contend with the stores across the road they likewise need to contend will every one of the web-based stores all over the planet that can give similar things, perhaps at additional cutthroat costs. Notwithstanding, a large number of studies shows that individuals will put brand devotion over cost. For your business, this implies that utilizing customer support to fabricate trust and devotion will pay off by holding customer's. The familiar maxim that finding new customers is multiple times more costly than keeping old ones turns out as expected. Through great customer care, you can keep any customer from being disappointed in any capacity that would provoke them to get back at you. Consumer loyalty is great assurance from unavoidable missteps gathering momentum into something a lot bigger and more hazardous.

•It Helps Memorability: In the age of the Web, verbal exchange spreads quickly. Individuals will regard a business with better customer care, and this could prompt a large number of additional customer's through only a couple of fulfilled customers posting a positive survey on the web.

Purchasers will decide on commonality and faithfulness over a lower cost. By being focused on the customer's, you are opening doors with the expectation of complimentary, promoting from fulfilled customer's. Individuals will make reference to your image name in discussion in a positive light, and a decent standing method.

Watching out for consumer loyalty will assist with recognizing issues and regions for development from the get go. Little things, such as refreshing connection points or changing the design of a store, can enormously affect consumer loyalty and are generally simple to achieve. Organizations are just kept alive by their customer's, so being focused on the fulfillment of those customers will assist your organization with becoming adaptable and dynamic enough to keep going for quite a while.

Organizations face a ton of progress today. In any case, there is continuously something to be said about focusing on it to treat customers well and declining to compromise in customer care.

Consumer loyalty is both the best assurance from botches and the best promotion for your business.

CHAPTER 6: MANAGING LOSING A CUSTOMER.

In the turbulent oceans of business, the certainty of losing a customer is a reality that each organization should confront. Dealing with this undeniable viewpoint requires a fragile touch, a mix of sympathy, key reasoning, and a guarantee to consistent improvement. Losing a customer is not just a transactional loss; it's an emotional one too. The first step in managing this process is acknowledging the emotional toll it can take on both parties involved. A long-standing relationship is more than a series of purchases; it's a connection built on trust, shared experiences, and mutual understanding.

A human-driven approach starts with compassion. Come at the situation from the customers perspective and grasp their purposes behind leaving. Was it disappointment with the item or administration? A change in needs or financial plan imperatives? By getting a handle on the close to home underpinnings, organizations can fit their reactions to meet the exceptional necessities of each leaving customer. Make a place of refuge for open correspondence. Urge Customer's to share their input, positive or negative. Useful analysis can be priceless for course rectification, and keeping a channel for exchange might try and present a chance for maintenance or future cooperation. Direct an exhaustive examination of the explanations for the takeoff. Was it a particular issue, a cutthroat proposition, or an adjustment of the customer's conditions? By understanding the main drivers, organizations can refine their techniques, tending to trouble spots and fortifying their offer.

Exploring the waters of customer's misfortune isn't just a deal; it's a human encounter. By figuring out the profound scene, answering in a calculated way, and protecting connections past takeoff, organizations can change the certainty of customer misfortune into a chance for development and improvement. In the rhythmic movement of Customer's affiliations, the urgent lies in pushing toward takeoffs with a human touch and a guarantee to tireless development.

Motivations behind Why Your Free endeavors Loses customer's.

• Sad customer care understanding

•Your thing or organization failed to compare suspicions

•You didn't show the value

•Your business is clashing

•You don't acquire from your mistakes

•Your business systems are outdated

Method for getting away from this:

√ appalling customer's backing's: Start with an inside survey of the methodologies that direct your gathering. Lead interviews with client help chiefs and representatives. Recall that you're not searching for spoiled eggs or places to allocate fault; all things being equal, you ought to be searching for points of grinding.

Evaluate what organization strategies lead to client disappointment. What inner issues keep the reps from supporting customer's rapidly and really? Utilize this information to further develop your customer's assistance rehearses.

And bear in mind these three golden rules of customer service:

• Respond quickly.

• Acknowledge when a mistake is made and make it right.

- Treat the customer with respect and empathy.

Support your customer support team. Your team can't do their best work if they don't have the resources to do their jobs well.

So, give your customer service team the resources they need to provide your customers with excellent service. This includes the technical infrastructure and the autonomy to make choices that will benefit your business and support your customers.

Your business will reap the benefits of happier customers and happier employees!

✓Your product or service failed to meet expectations: Design and build a quality product or service. Your product or service should do what it claims to and do it well. Don't think that marketing magic or any other business trickery will make up for an inferior product or poorly executed service.

Therefore, work with an able item originator Test. Work with quality accouterments, Acclimate your administration in light of customer review. Take the necessary way to make and convey a help or item that graces pay for.

✓ Oversee hypotheticals: slanted hypotheticals can be hindering your business as a frail item. Anyhow of how superb your administration or item is, assuming that your guests were awaiting different, they wouldn't be cheerful.

Therefore, ensure you comprehend what your business' image guarantee truly is. What supposition for regard would you say you're making for your customer's?

Presently, articulate that brand guarantee and deal with the client experience to fully convey it.

✓ You did not show the worth: What astounding value do you bring to your Customer's that different associations don't? This is your one of a kind incitement.

An UVP plainly makes sense of how you'll attack your client's concern, the advantages included, and what separates your offer from the pack.

Taking the time to nail down your UVP internally will enable you to better explain the value to your customers.

Obviously understand your UVP on all stages. Distribute the advantages of your item or administration on your site. Teach your Customer care and deal with staff so they can talk smoothly about the worth remembered for your valuing. What's more, include your novel incentive on the presentation page for each deal.

Regardless of where your Customer meets your deal, the extraordinary incentive ought to be there, as well.

✓Your business is conflicting: Convey an encounter that customers can depend on. This begins with you and your representatives.

Instruct every one of your workers about what a decent customer experience ought to resemble.

Make a brand style manual for lay out uniform marking rules and offer it with your plan group and everybody liable for promoting content and materials.

Consider your workers responsible for conveying a reliably certain client experience.

Make solid customer cooperation arrangements. In the event that you have a discount strategy, consider it cautiously prior to sending it off. Do you offer trades? Store credit?

Anything your techniques are, ensure they will function admirably for your customer's before you execute them. Then, remain with them! Be consistent.

Rebrand, if fitting. Once in a while, the best methodology is to rebrand and make a more predictable, more grounded brand character.

√You don't gain from your slip-ups: Keep a functioning fixed presence. The web gives free criticism. Screen the most famous survey destinations and get some margin to circle back to disappointed customers. Exploit this public gathering to show that your organization will stand by listening to its customers and make things right.

Acknowledge negative customer input. Pay attention to grumblings and acclimate to work on your item or administration. This will assist you with clutching upset customers, work on your business, item, or administration, and make a superior encounter for everybody. Numerous internet based overview instruments offer ways of catching criticism, assisting you with rapidly recognizing issues.

√ Your business strategies are obsolete: Utilize esteem based selling procedures. Carve out opportunities to realize what your customer needs. Then, at that point, offer worthwhile arrangements that address those requirements. Show how your item helps the customer and permit them to choose if it fits them.

Assemble associations with your Customer's, On the off chance that you're attempting to sell with each and every customer association, you're treating it terribly. All things being equal, center around laying out entrust with your imminent customer's.

Have legit collaborations and offer some benefit through supportive substance and engaging web-based entertainment commitment. Then, at that point, when a customer needs the item or administration you give - they'll go to you, they confide in the asset.

Keep an eye on your herd

The way to grow a business is keeping up with your customer's while obtaining new ones.

In this way, quit spilling customer's.

An issue you haven't distinguished is as yet an issue. In this way, really investigate the regions where your business might miss the mark.

Then, at that point, make the important moves to cure the issues you find.

Inspect your customer's support arrangements and your item or administration itself. Where might they at any point move along?

Could you at any point better show the worth and give a more steady customer experience? Then do it!

Could it be said that you are neglecting customer input? Do you utilize obsolete deals procedures?

Your business development relies upon it.

CHAPTER 7: KINDS OF CUSTOMER'S NECESSITIES.

✓ Transparency: It is an approach to demonstrating to clients or potential clients that your business has no great explanation not to show precisely exact things occurring inside your business. Straightforwardness helps clients, yet it additionally helps organizations with regards to keeping up with validity.

Importance of Transparency

•It Build Trust: As expressed over perhaps the greatest way straightforwardness can help your business is on the grounds that it fabricates trust. Recall things you have purchased or put resources into before. How much exploration did you do? Assuming there were awful surveys, did that influence you from buying it? These inquiries are precisely the exact thing your client's go through in their minds when they purchase something too. In case your customer's trust your business, they will undoubtedly place assets into your things.

•Stronger Relationship. Straightforwardness assists fabricate more grounded associations with your customer's and with your representatives. Representatives will have more trust in the administration and the choices that are being made inside the organization since they know precisely the exact thing is occurring and why it is working out. This makes them pleased with the organization they are working for and feel like their work implies something.

Straightforwardness additionally empowers better correspondence all through the work environment. This prompts more inventive and imaginative thoughts, better criticism, and so on in light of the fact that representatives feel enabled to share their thoughts. This harvests more grounded better connections representative to workers too.

Your customer's and your business will have a more grounded relationship since you can be very legitimate with them since you don't have anything to stow away. This will build your deals and assist with holding your customer base.

•increases productivity. At the point when the executive is really straightforward about its vision and mission, it can have serious areas of strength to construct and entrust with its workers. Representatives then likewise know precisely the exact thing they are working for and why it is significant. With that responsibility and inspiration driving them, they are progressively more useful. ✓ Quality: Business quality is a proportion of how well an organization addresses the issues and assumptions for its clients. It depends on consumer loyalty studies,

Great quality administration can improve your association's image and notoriety, safeguard it against chances, increment its proficiency, help its benefits and decrease waste, and position it to continue to develop.

IMPORTANCE OF QUALITY

- Brand image: Customers assess the quality of a product with the brand image of a company.

- Quality helps in managing costs effectively

- Appearance: The look of the product is an important measure for fashion apparel.

✓Information: In the data age, organizations that outfit the force of information are better situated to flourish. Business data isn't only a device; a powerful power pushes associations forward. Whether it's directing choices, molding systems, encouraging development, overseeing gambles, or advancing cooperative societies, the job of business data is essential to the progress of ventures in the present unique business scene. As organizations keep on advancing, the people who embrace the groundbreaking capability of data will without a doubt lead the way into what's in store.

The compelling administration and usage of data stand as mainstays of progress. Whether you're a startup holding back nothing, a laid out big business exploring industry moves, the meaning of business data couldn't possibly be more significant.

✓ Assortment of choices: The specialty of pursuing grouped decisions in business isn't tied in with looking for a solitary, faultless tune yet about making a dynamic and versatile structure that reverberates with the steadily changing elements of the market. Embracing the variety of decisions, organizations can explore vulnerabilities, benefit from valuable open doors, and make a story out of supported achievement.

✓ Dependability and Manageability: The Foundation of Trust

At the core of each and every flourishing business is the bedrock of trust, and constancy is its foundation. For Customer's, providers, and partners the same, the confirmation that responsibilities will be regarded and assumptions met is central. Constancy reaches out past item quality, it incorporates the dependability of administrations, conveyance timetables, and the steady satisfaction of commitments.

Steadfastness and sensibility are not independent, their collaboration makes a considerable starting point for progress. A reliable business moves trust, and reasonability guarantees that this trust is reliably maintained. This unique pair is particularly basic in the present quick moving and eccentric business landscape. Consider a monetary organization overseeing client speculations. The reliability of exact monetary data and straightforward correspondence lays out entrust with clients. All the while, the reasonability of powerful gamble the executives' frameworks and consistency strategies shields both the customer's advantages and the establishment's honesty. Together, reliability and sensibility make a versatile biological system that can weather conditions storms and exploit open doors.

While reliability sets the stage, sensibility starts to lead the pack in arranging the complicated ensemble of business tasks. Sensibility includes making frameworks and cycles that smooth out work processes, streamline assets, and adjust to evolving conditions. A successfully overseen business isn't simply productive yet in addition versatile even with difficulties.

CHAPTER 8: RESULTS OF INDISCRETION.

The waves of rashness stretch out a long way past the prompt demonstration, impacting connections, notoriety, and, surprisingly, one's healthy identity. Understanding the results is fundamental for the two people and society at large.

With regards to individual connections, the results of rashness can be significant. Trust, once broken, turns into a sensitive string that requires fastidious consideration to fix. The profound cost for all gatherings included can be persevering, requiring a sensitive course of mending and modifying

Effects of indiscretion

✓ Harm to Trust: One of the most prompt and significant results of careless activities is the disintegration of trust. Whether in private connections, proficient settings, or cultural settings, demonstrations of carelessness can break the underpinning of trust that people and foundations depend on. Reconstructing trust frequently demands huge investment, exertion, and predictable exhibit of changed conduct.

✓ Strained Relationships: Careless activities, especially in private connections, can strain the close to home connections between people. Treachery, untrustworthiness, or breaks of certainty can prompt profound torment, disdain, and a feeling of selling out. Revamping connections post carelessness requests open correspondence, true conciliatory sentiments.

✓ Emotional and Psychological Toll: Thoughtless activities frequently negatively affect a person's close to home and mental prosperity. Responsibility, disgrace, and regret can become dependable friends, influencing psychological wellness and in general life fulfillment.

10 Way's out of Indiscretions

1. **Affirmation and Acknowledgment:** Begin by recognizing your slip-up and tolerating liability regarding your activities. Abstain from rationalizing or accusing others. This sets the establishment for authentic regret.

2. **Open Correspondence:** Participate in transparent correspondence with the impacted party. Talk about your thoughts, express regret, and be open to their viewpoint. Clear correspondence lays the basis for understanding and goal.

3. **Compassion:** Show sympathy by attempting to comprehend what your activities might have meant for the other individual inwardly. This shows that you are truly worried about their sentiments and ready to imagine their perspective.

4. **Apologize Genuinely:** Offer an earnest expression of remorse, stressing the particular activities that caused the carelessness. A certified statement of regret mirrors your regret and obligation to set things right. Stay away from conventional or unscrupulous expressions of remorse.

5. **Resolve to Change:** Express your obligation to change and blueprint explicit advances you will take to forestall a repeat. Exhibiting a proactive way to deal with self-improvement can assist with revamping trust.

6. **Look for Proficient Assistance if Vital:** at times, looking for the help of a specialist or instructor can give a nonpartisan space to the two players to investigate issues and work towards a goal. Proficient direction can be instrumental in the mending system.

7. **Gain from the Experience:** Utilize tactlessness as a chance for self-awareness. Ponder the hidden purposes for your activities and consider what you can gain from the experience to improve personally.

8.   **Reconstructing Trust:** Revamping trust takes time and reliable exertion. Be patient and comprehend the other individual's sentiments. Little, reliable activities that line up with your obligation to change can add to reconstructing trust.

9.   **Lay out Limits:** Obviously characterize and regard limits to forestall comparable thoughtless activities later on. Straightforwardly talk about assumptions and cutoff points in the relationship to guarantee the two players have a solid sense of safety.

10.   **Keep up with Straightforwardness:** Straightforwardness is vital in revamping trust. Be open about your activities, whereabouts, and goals. This helps cultivate a climate of trustworthiness and decreases the probability of false impressions.

Keep in mind, every circumstance is one of a kind, and the viability of these methodologies might shift. Moving toward the interaction with truthfulness, patience is fundamental.

CHAPTER 9: HOW WOULD YOU DEFEAT A CUSTOMER'S INDISCRETION.

Detachment doesn't imply that the customer's could do without what they're getting from you or your organization overall. All things considered, customer's unresponsiveness is the point at which your customers are not amped up for your image and couldn't care less about who's giving them the assistance. Unresponsive customers are eager to move to a contending brand in the event that the proposition is better and the exchange costs are sufficiently low.

Faithfulness and aloofness are not viable. It is beyond the realm of possibilities for customer's to remain faithful to your business assuming they are unresponsive, uninterested, or separated from you and your image. Customer's that vibe like your item, administration, or organization are effectively replaceable are not the sort of customer's you need to have. Stopping customer detachment from ever really developing can assist you with building a superior standing for your business, long haul customer connections, and solid organization attached with key records.

•**Observe Achievements:** Recognize and celebrate customer achievements, like commemorations or accomplishments. This adds an individual touch and reinforces the profound association between the customer and your image.

•**Openness:** Guarantee that customer's can without much of a stretch contact you through different channels. Openness adds to a positive customer experience and decreases disappointment.

•**Proactive Issue Goal:** Expect possible issues and address them proactively. Stepping up and determining issues before they heighten can improve consumer loyalty.

•**Adjust to customer's Patterns:** Stay delicate to create customer examples and tendencies. Changing your commitments considering these examples shows that you are open to changing client needs.

•**Community Engagement:** Encourage a feeling of local area around your image. Urge customers to share their encounters and make a space for them to interface with one another.

•**Surprise and Delight:** At times shock customer's with startling advantages or rewards. This can make a positive and significant experience, starting reestablished interest.

•**Educational Content:** Give important and instructive substance connected with your items or administrations. This illuminates customer's as well as draws in them, encouraging a feeling of association.

•**Nonstop Improvement:** Exhibit a guarantee to consistent improvement. Tell customers about updates, upgrades, or changes in view of their criticism.

•**Clear Correspondence:** Guarantee your correspondence is clear and straightforward. Uncertainty can prompt disarray and disappointment, adding to client lack of care.

•**Reward Dependability:** Execute a reliability program to remunerate customer's for their recurrent business. Impetuses can go from limits to restrictive access or customized offers.

•**Surveys and Feedback:** Execute customer reviews to accumulate criticism. Follow up on the bits of knowledge acquired from these reviews to work on your items or administrations in view of customer inclinations.

•**Brief Reactions:** Answer quickly to customer requests or concerns. Speedy reactions exhibit your obligation to tending to their requirements and worries sooner rather than later.

•**Customized Communications:** Designer your associations to every customer. Perceive their singular inclinations and history with your item or administration. Personalization assists customers with feeling seen and appreciated.

•Undivided attention: Find opportunity to pay attention to your customer's effectively. Grasp their interests, inclinations, and criticism. This shows that you esteem their feedback and are mindful of their requirements.

CONCLUSION

The hazards of recklessness act as a distinct wake up call of the potential outcomes that can unfurl when we disregard scrupulousness and dismissal the effect of our activities. Whether in private connections, proficient undertakings, or everyday assignments, remissness can raise errors, disintegrate trust, and lead to accidental mischief. As we explore the intricacies of life, it becomes basic to perceive the meaning of careful thought in the most natural sounding way for us, choices, and communications. The expanding influences of lack of regard reach out a long ways past the quick second, impacting the elements of our associations and the results of our endeavors.To relieve these risks, we should develop an increased feeling of mindfulness, embracing a mentality that values accuracy, responsibility, and sympathy. Thus, we not just defend ourselves from the traps of imprudence yet in addition to the production of an additional kind and empathetic world.

Basically, let us track with careful advances, understanding that our meticulousness and principles can be the remedy to the risks that hide in the shadows of recklessness. Through this purposeful methodology, we make ready for significant associations, positive results, and a future where the repercussions of our activities reverberate with the reverberation of reasonability and mindfulness.

REVIEW

Dear (Recipient's)

I hope this message finds you well. I am writing to request your thoughtful review and feedback on a piece I've recently crafted on the topic of "The Perils of Carelessness." Your insights are invaluable to me, and I believe your perspective will contribute significantly to the refinement of this work. The essay delves into the consequences of carelessness in various aspects of life, from personal relationships to professional endeavors. It emphasizes the need for mindfulness, accountability, and empathy as essential antidotes to the perils that may arise from neglecting attention to detail.

I am particularly interested in your thoughts on the overall coherence of the piece, the effectiveness of the conclusion, and any suggestions you might have for improvement. Your expertise and discerning eye would be immensely beneficial as I strive to convey the message with clarity and impact.

Please feel free to provide your feedback at your earliest convenience. I am open to any constructive criticism and appreciate your time and consideration in advance.

Thank you for your invaluable input, and I look forward to hearing your thoughts.

Warm regards,

(Felecia.B.brown)